D1077655

Celebrating the Quaker Way

Ben Pink Dandelion

For all of us

Second edition

Second edition,

Published May 2010 by Quaker Books,

Friends House, 173 Euston Road, London NW1 2BJ

www.quaker.org.uk

Enquiries should be addressed to Quaker Books,
Quaker Communications, Friends House, 173 Euston Road,
London NW1 2BJ

www.quaker.org.uk

Printed by Hastings Printing Company Ltd

ISBN 978 1 907123 13 9

FSC

Recycled
Supporting responsible use
of forest resources

Cert no. TT-COC-002609
www.fsc.org
© 1996 Forest Stewardship Council

Foreword

The trustees of The Joseph Rowntree Charitable Trust have commissioned this short devotional work to help us describe and celebrate the Quaker way that we know and practise in Britain Yearly Meeting, and which is practised elsewhere. This is a form of worship which is sometimes termed 'liberal' or 'unprogrammed', to distinguish it from evangelical or programmed worship found in other parts of the world; however the heart of this book is for all those who enjoy open worship as part of their Quaker experience and who seek to live their lives as Friends.

It is a Quaker way that we are familiar with, and from which we derive great strength, comfort and challenge, but one that is hard to describe. We feel it draws us together, closer to God and to God's purposes, giving us a place to stand, an understanding of how to live our lives. What we share together goes deeper than words.

But it is vital that we find these words – for our own clarity of understanding, for the enlightenment of others and for the growth of our meetings. Where we should be eloquent, we often find ourselves tongue-tied. In a religious society without trained ministers, the task of attempting to speak what we know and understand of the nature and purposes of God falls to each one of us, not just a few. It is something we all need to encourage in each other.

We are deeply grateful for what Ben has produced. What he has written comes to us in his own voice, and the voices of Friends he has spoken to. We offer it in the hope that it will be widely read, and will inspire each of us to find our own voice, to speak passionately to each other of what we know, to express the power we find in the experience of our Quaker faith, to be God's ministers in the world today.

Marion McNaughton
Chair of Trustees
Joseph Rowntree Charitable Trust

Introduction

This pocket-sized book celebrates the Quaker way and affirms the wonderful riches of the Quaker tradition in Britain, and the Quaker 'Liberal tradition' more widely. It is a book for Quakers rather than about them. It talks of 'us' and 'we' and is for 'insiders'. It is a devotional book, for us.

I talk of God in the way Friends have traditionally talked of the divine, although some today may prefer other terms, and I hope that those readers can 'translate' or hear where the words come from, as they might approach ministry in meeting for worship. I write as a Quaker who came to meeting as an atheist/agnostic, drawn in by the peace testimony, an ex-anarchist, happy to find another place without leaders and without votes. Two years in, I had an experience aboard a Greyhound bus in America that gave me a sense of being lifted up, held, and since then perpetually accompanied by what I call God, but which I know is ultimately a mystery that it is not for me to know too closely. Thus, my being a Quaker moved from a primarily political affiliation to a place where I could connect and reconnnect with that grace-filled sense of being watched over, guarded and guided. It has fitted me not only intellectually but practically in my life of faith. It gives me exactly the form of worship and the opportunity for expression and service that matches my own experience of direct inward encounter.

We all have a ministry, or a series of ministries, each for its season, where we use the spiritual gifts given us by God. This book is written as part of my ministry. It draws on my Quaker experience, all I have heard and read in these last decades, and some twenty conversations conducted especially for the book (these Friends' words are in quotation marks). I trust I have been faithful to what has been given me.

I begin by suggesting what it means to call ourselves Quaker. The second part is more reflective, and I celebrate the nature of silent worship and its transforming potential, vocal ministry, discernment, and community. In the third part I explore the call to action following on from our direct relationship with God, our 'testimony'.

1   I am a Quaker

I am a Quaker. I am part of a worldwide Quaker community
and I inhabit that knowledge daily. It helps me live the way
I want to. The knowledge and reality of that community
membership informs my life and gives me the strength I need
to live faithfully, to speak truth to power, to witness in the
world.

I feel different from those around me, and my faith impels me
to live a different life from the one the secular world tells me I
should. As I walk down the street, catch the bus, take the train,
drive, eat, speak, or buy, I am not following society's norms,
but those alternative ones hewn out by Quakers over three and
a half centuries of discerning what is called from us as a people
of God. I feel clothed in my faith.

That witness is not about hats and tithes now, but it is still
about not deferring to those in positions of power, about
treating all of humanity equally, about not supporting
institutions that perpetuate wrong thinking or wrongdoing. It
is about speaking out and living 'out' for justice and peace, and
the integrity of creation.

Our testimony is about simplicity over commercialism,
materialism and greed. It is about having what we need
rather than what we want. It is about the integrity of all over
hierarchy and competition and the exploitation of people for
profit. It is about promoting peace, not war. It is about not
seeing war as a means to any end. It is about community, not

individualism. It is about stewardship, not short-term gain. It is all about living faithfully, not for ourselves but for the greater good. Testimony is about attempting God's will. It is about living a life for justice in the world, not only among us. And as Quakers, wonderfully, we do not have to do these things alone.

Our Quaker identity and community supports us when we are in the world and countering its assumptions, and it informs and changes our lives. It helps me in the stands I want to make and it helps me see others I should be making. A core set of values and principles travels with me and through me, so that my lif may preach. I am given support and inspiration, aspiration and affirmation.

When I am wrestling with an issue, I can take it to my Quaker friends, my Quaker network, my Quaker meeting. I can seek 'clearness' informally or formally. I can help others 'discern'. I can find help interpreting my sense of what God wants of me, and what that may mean in any particular situation. My knowledge of the presence of such a community in itself gives support and guidance. The well-known stories of Quaker action in the world, of reaction to the unforeseen, of resolve against the odds, of response to the dangerous and hostile, give me tools to mould and shape my own responses. I am both held by the community and am part of the holding – holding others as they discern, holding the tradition as we discern, holding the future of the Quaker way in a group that has no leaders but ourselves, no 'them' but us.

And I know that this desire to get my life right is a priority for me, but also is a shared priority. I know that others will listen to learn, and share what they already know so that I may learn. For all of us, these things matter enormously. We are friends as well as Friends, and we are friends with the shared purpose and desire to get our lives right.

This friendship transcends geography. It is wider than my immediate neighbourhood, stretches farther than my meeting's boundary, beyond the confines of any one yearly meeting and any one language. My Quaker belonging is about being part of a global network of those I have met, sat on committees with, worshipped with, discerned with. We have worked together and prayed together. We have washed pots, raked leaves, sat in meetings for hours or committees for days. We have known each other in the things which have felt eternal, as well as those things which truly are. We have slept on floors in meeting houses as Young Friends, stayed up all night talking excitedly, experimented with worship, and had our hearts linked and broken along the way. We have travelled to visit each other, knowing that we will find a welcome and a like mind at the end of the journey. We have known that, as long as we stay within the Quaker fold, we will most likely meet again. It is a companionship of the greatest depth and trust. These are friendships 'for life' in every sense.

Often nothing needs to be spoken. Silently, we share a reaction to a news item, to a beggar in the street, to a billboard advertisement, or to a choice of product in a supermarket.

At other times, we can joyfully disagree and argue in love to see the other's view, to decide together what it is best to do. We may continue to disagree, but most often what is shared outweighs what is not. We are able to continue living alongside one another 'up the mountain' of our collective affiliation to the Religious Society of Friends.

All the time, we are galvanised more and more to action. The repeated urgings of the faithful Friend, the mailings from Yearly Meeting, or an article in the Quaker press at any point may strike the seasoned nerve, and move us from concern to action. After one successful demonstration, the next feels all the easier. We become old hands at being creative in our dealings with the establishment. We drive food aid to refugees, blockade nuclear bases, worship outside early warning defence establishments, petition and lobby, talk and persuade. And even when we are not successful at this moment, the seed can be planted from which the next generation can draw nourishment and support.

We, as Quakers, have long traditions of work against slavery and for penal reform started by pioneers amongst us, those who were not always listened to, but who nevertheless created a legacy we have been able to join and follow. If we are not listened to today, we can have the hope that we may be pioneers for tomorrow's Quakers.

We know we may not be right, but we also know that what matters most is the faithful seeking that informs all we do. We do not always have the solutions, but we know we are sometimes given 'incredible answers' to questions we have. When we come together, we find community and acceptance in our worship and together discern dreams we never imagined we could have, and ones we never could have had on our own. In that place of holy discovery, beyond reason, we can find divinely inspired solutions that we could never have found by logic alone. Such is the art of discernment, the art of the holy.

We know for ourselves that we have found a spiritual community that is the best place for us to sit within for now. For many of us, it has been a 'homecoming'. It is a place for us to live our lives, to position our lives within this tradition and all its insights, and a place from which to continue our journey. It is not a place that claims to have all the answers but one which rather encourages questions. It is a spiritual home which emphasises seeking and which is cautious about finally finding. It is a spiritual home which encourages us to make our own choices, to live by our own interpretations of the tradition and its current understandings, a place to work out for ourselves what a Quaker life may look like.

It gives us the tradition to guide us, that legacy of past understandings, and a set of amazing tools to help us get it right for now: worship; an understanding of worshipping community; a discernment process; and, ultimately, the ability to make whatever we will of what we have, to become whoever we choose to be as a people of faith regardless of the past or present.

This freedom is also a responsibility, and it is right and wonderful that we undertake this journey together. 'I am a Quaker' is not an individualistic statement, it is a declaration of community. It is to declare our spiritual values, here and now in this community, and our endeavour to live a life within and alongside those values. It is to discern within and against the tradition. What a wonderful gift it is to be a Quaker.

2   Meeting

Worship

Come into the silence of a Quaker meeting. Outward quiet
gives us the inward place of amazing opportunity and
fantastical connection. 'Sink down to the seed' and we find we
inhabit a new space, out of 'the world', away from the earthly
and secular, that touches heaven and allows us to find and
feel God. Absence leads to Presence. This is an intentional
silence, a deliberate attempt to feel connection, additional to
the incidental divine accompaniment we can feel at any time
in any week.

We sit in a tradition of revolutionary discovery: a discovery
of the power found within the silence that transforms lives,
that transforms communities of believers, that transforms
the world through the call to action that emerges within that
inward relationship.

What happens to us in the silence varies but we know its
power and its value. We know that it works, that it gives us a
doorway into the mystery of faith. We know that the unique
Quaker form of worship is the place, the wonderful place, we
find we need to be.

The silence of worship is not just an absence of noise, or even
an outward stilling of the physical, it is a journey within, a
'going inside' to a deeply felt but easily reached place of holy

relationship. Together, we meet each other in the silence, come together, 'all focusing on something we share', 'picking up the same questions in the silence', gathered, before God. We come expectantly and in surrender. We come in the hope of we know not what, the hope of faith. We come in the humility of those seeking, those grateful for what we are given, those hungry to hear the call, those eager to work with God to further God's loving purposes. We come as those who know that the world is not as loving as it might be, that humanity hurts itself as well as the planet, that we need to at least try doing our bit to help, and that our faith both requires this of us, and helps us achieve what we discern is best.

We come too with our own sense of brokenness, of shortcomings, and failures and fallings short. We come with our own need to be in right relationship with each other and with the divine, our own need of help and accompaniment. We come with our own desire to feel again and again the magic and grace of God's love in our lives, of God's wisdom alongside our thinking, of God's faith in us as we struggle from time to time with our faith in God or in ourselves.

Thus our times of worship, whether alone at home or at meeting, feed us and our faith while also representing our response to the mystery of the divine. We sit in the silence, open to God and opening to God. God is there and we continue the silence in awe and wonder, in adoring prayer and gratitude for all we have been given. We 'bathe in the silence' and it 'feels right, just right'.

14

'A few weeks ago, I wasn't well enough to come. Come the hour, I sat down and thought "I'm going to sit here quietly, this is my hour when I should be at meeting" and I was alone, but I sat quietly, just emptied my mind, and suddenly I didn't feel alone, I was sure there was something happening at meeting and I felt it, and I didn't feel alone for that hour, I was greatly comforted.'

The beauty of silence is that it allows us to engage where we are. We are not dovetailed into someone else's sermon, neither are our devotions determined by an outward liturgy. Rather, our motions of faith can sit where they need to be, close to us in their authenticity and sincerity, closer to God in their directness and individuality. 'Let Love be the first motion': the motivating and originating love of our outward life and witness sits as a reflection of our impulse towards love within. It is a personal motion of love, for ourselves, for our friends, for God, for the 'complete place' of unity with the divine that we discover in that inward and outward silence.

We review our lives. We pray. We hold in the Light. We think. We feel connected, refreshed, accepted. We walk with our guide. We hand things over to God. We trust. We find faith need not be total. We see that hope is more important than belief. We feel. We go beyond reason, to where it feels as if the whole of life is God. We find nothing between us and God. Life becomes prayer.

I write as if this encounter with God and personal transformation is automatic and easy. It is not, of course, and many of us sit in meeting still hoping to feel God's presence. Maybe we have, and have not recognised it. Maybe God's invitation has not yet come to us. Between those moments of gathered intensity, we learn, sometimes painfully, to wait hopefully and expectantly. As Quakers, as part of a tradition founded and sustained on direct inward encounter, we know that an experience of the divine can and does come regularly to thousands of Friends. That knowledge may not make it easier for those of us still seeking, but it can turn a potentially pessimistic and cynical atheism into an optimistic agnosticism. Believing it is worth seeking was the original impulse that led George Fox not only to his despair but also to his critical experience of encounter and truth.

For some of us, often it is outside of meeting that God feels closest, or that we feel more 'in the right place with God'. I call these times 'holy moments', when everything feels aligned and congruent. For me, they have often come walking the streets of London, where the aesthetic of the outward architecture, the richness of life on the street around me, the delicacy of the cuisine on offer, or the arc of a particularly graceful classic motor car, calls forth the joy and thanksgiving deep within my soul at being a part of this holy landscape. Indeed, given my perpetual sense of accompaniment and the joy that goes with it, I feel God close at hand almost everywhere I choose to be truly open.

Going to meeting, then, is about intentionality and about communal sacramental connection. There, I join with others to experience 'communion after the manner of Friends'. It is powerful and wonderful. It is the inward supper. There is something very important and precious about the regularity and routine of the discipline of deliberateness. It is a discipline of remaining aware of the relationship with God, of putting it first, of knowing that, particularly when it feels least helpful, or when we feel least deserving, this time of intentional expectancy, and the hope that underpins it, is exactly what is required.

There is something to be treasured in the routines and rituals of Quaker meeting. There is familiarity but also the remembrance to ourselves of the desire to set time aside to concentrate on what is alongside us at all times but often hidden from us by our busyness. 'Keeping the pace' as well as the peace of our lives does not override the need to deliberately give ourselves times of intentional intimacy with God. 'My Quakerism lives in my local meeting – always the place I come back to, and want to come back to.'

Ministry

The direct relationship we experience with God leads to a continued spiritual intimacy. Nobody and nothing needs to be between ourselves and the divine: we are all raised up to work alongside and for God's loving purposes in and over 'the world.' Each of us is a precious child of God and is given ministry, a spiritual gift or gifts to share freely and faithfully with and beyond the community. Quaker faith is about doing and not just being. It may begin with the individual but it is never private.

Silence within the Quaker setting is used for the approach to God but also as the medium for discerning the action we are called to take individually and corporately. In and through the silence, we are gathered and guided by God. Wary of explicit theology, we make silence our approach to God and also our response, a symbol of our particular attitude towards not knowing, or feeling not able to say too much in particular, about the mystery of the divine.

Cautious about speech, we are concerned that our attempts to transmit something of our experience fall short or demean the experience we are trying to convey. We meet in silence, discern and offer ministry, and let it be received in silence. It may look like an arid loop but it rests totally on the unmediated experience of the divine, unbidden but continually available, the personal and corporate discernment of that experience, and ministry in silence as well as speech. Ministry may be given in 'entire and trustful silence alone'; words may be unnecessary to convey what God is giving us to share. Equally, others sometimes speak exactly what is on our hearts.

Vocal ministry is different from everyday talk. Ministry may be 'more eloquent than everyday speech' or feel very specific: 'there is a pounding, shaking, I feel forced – my voice disappears, I have only the vaguest idea of what I am going to say, only a vague idea of what I've said'; 'something stays in my head, won't go away, then an angle on it will come, then the words – it becomes very difficult to breathe, but I say it and calm down, nothing comes in afterwards, very often I don't remember what was said.'

'Just thinking about it makes me shake … I feel terrified, … it's exposing yourself … exhilarating but also terrifying … if I had a choice, I would stay sat down.'

We are vessels. It is not our ministry but we need to be faithful to the leadings we are given. 'Water tastes of the pipes – vocal ministry works with my experience but comes through me.'

We are not islands, neither should we try to be for little do we know the consequences and impact of our own actions. When we are advised to come to meeting regardless of how we feel, that sage advice is not just for our own welfare but for whosoever we may meet that day. The ministry we are led to give may not be for us or even the majority of the meeting, yet the 'wonderful book of discipline' reminds us that it may be for somebody. I once heard as a 'ministry' someone advertise a video they had been involved in producing. They even gave the price and how to order it. On my high Quaker horse, I sat there amazed at what might count as ministry, and then was chastened by a flow of the most unexpectedly insightful and powerful ministry, all springing from the video being about bereavement, and the word having found life in the silence of meeting.

Whether or not we minister vocally in meeting, we all have a ministry. To say we have a gift or a particular ministry is to say nothing at all about our human self but merely to reflect on something given us by God for a purpose: 'ministry is a gift to me to share with the meeting'. As it says in 1 Corinthians 12, we all have different gifts and we all have our part to play. The test of authenticity is found in the fruits of the spirit and in the building of community.

In a permissive Quakerism, we decide what is appropriate, what is Quaker for us, how we interpret our Quaker faith in day-to-day life. We no longer look and sound different from the rest of the population, as the earlier Friends did with their Quaker grey and insistence on 'thee' and 'thou', numbering days and months instead of using their pagan names. The sense of difference between us and those whose behaviours we wish to challenge, as with our faith, is now an inward affair. And so, equally, is the challenge, to live that difference inwardly, to 'know' it intimately and to live our lives in that spirit, still as co-agents with God.

Discernment

In a faith which claims God speaks to us directly, knowing what is of God is crucial and we require reliable access to that experience for guidance in daily life.

In practice, we come to know what is in 'right ordering' within our lives, perhaps through finding we have got things wrong, or feeling the fruits of the spirit that emerge, ultimately developing a sense of alignment or congruence or 'instinct' when we are getting it right.

It may mean we need to 'find somewhere quiet and stop'.
'Home becomes a place of prayer – I open the curtains with a
prayer, wake up in the night with a prayer … have a cup of tea
with God.' 'I pray about all decisions and get to a picture, an
image, … sometimes just become clear having prayed about it.'
There is a sense of 'flow' or 'energy' when we have clarity, and
one of being 'out of kilter' when we do not.

We can all encounter God directly. We can all experience
God's guidance and we can all minister that to the group.
We use the same basis for our business meetings: expectant
waiting and ministry which comes out of the silence. It is
worship with a theme, and for some of us, Quaker business
method is the most visible and reliable symbol of direct
encounter. In one committee there have been 'lots of practical
things to do but they are interspersed with an explicit feeling
that what we are doing is God's work.' Yearly Meeting with
its gatherings of over one thousand Friends is particularly
affirming of our faith and practice. Large numbers of us
regularly and reliably find a 'sense of the meeting' and we
move forward on major decisions. We are well practised at
discernment and it is a communal gift we should celebrate
more explicitly.

So discernment, deciding what is of God and what is not, is
the most visible role of the gathered meeting but also its most
fundamental. It is the most crucial exercise of a church which
claims its authority and wisdom is found in corporate direct
encounter over and against text or tradition. The gathered

meeting decides for itself what is truly from God, no book, leader, or part of the past. Our future is in our discernment.

Community

Quakerism has never been about going it alone. Numbers bring reliability in terms of Quaker discernment and political strength in trying to change the world, but there is something more fundamental in being 'gathered as in a net', the human desire and need to relate. I have talked with ex-Quakers, many of whom still feel they are Quaker but that the local or national meeting has lost its Quaker way. There is nowhere else for these grieving Quakers to go and so many sit at home and worship on their own. No one can test their leadings or unite with their concerns. No one is there to accompany them on their faith journey, to be alongside, to help with pastoral needs or the nurture of their ministry, other than God alone. This I suggest is not how God or Quakerism imagines a life of faith. Rather, community is at the heart of Quaker worship and of Quaker discernment. We don't need to be all in the same place for prayer and worship to feel powerfully connected but knowing when others are also engaged in these ways can have a great effect.

'People praying on a topic is powerful, not physically together but wherever they are, we don't need our bodies to be in the same place … I learn and relearn about faith, I really need not to worry, to trust in God, and give it to God and not grab it back … just trust that the right thing will happen.'

Our structures reflect and nurture this joint dependence on each other and on God. We are all spiritually equal, all part of the 'priesthood'. We can all attend business meetings and should do. We share the tasks that need to be done to remain an effective worship group, and rotate them. We are all responsible financially. We are all responsible practically. We are all responsible spiritually, all elders and overseers to each other and the meeting, all nurturing and caring for the community.

Often it is the less formal moments that build community most. My meeting has loved its days of bench-waxing or railing-painting, and in a previous meeting regular day-long walks attracted not only a high proportion of those who turn up on Sunday but their non-Quaker family and friends. Having fewer named posts in my meeting has helped more people to come forward, and reminds me of the meeting in Chicago where, in crisis over nominations, they scrapped all the formal structure and began again with a list of immediate needs. Volunteers come forward when the tasks have life: 'The Holy Spirit took me by the hand'. We are bound together by the processes and the fruits of our discernment.

Our worship witnesses to the radical and unique form of Quaker liturgy, an unmediated and direct alternative within a religious world still dominated by the rule of expertise, ministers and mediators, personal and textual authority. Quaker business meeting witnesses to the power of collective spiritual experience in seeking God's guidance on any matter.

The minutes and epistles that emerge from these meetings are witness not only to their content but to a process that continues to subvert the secular hierarchies of the status quo. The book of discipline, reviewed in each generation, is testimony to the Quaker search for truth, the experience of continuing revelation, and that God requires us to take on new roles and emphases in each age. All witness to our rich corporate tradition and that we are, powerfully and practically, Quakers together.

3 Testimony

The direct encounter with the mystery of the divine at the heart of Quaker faith demands not only the response of worship and continued expectant waiting but an active demonstration of the insights God gives us. In other words, we are not given guidance that is private only to us either in its scope or in its application. Faith is about action in the world.

This witness to God's imperatives working through us has been traditionally labelled by Quakers as 'testimony'. What we call a testimony to the grace of God in the life of a deceased Friend is our witness to that grace which was so obvious in how they lived.

Similarly as our lives preach of God's loving purposes and work towards their fulfilment, so that witness is referred to as our testimony.

Today we may see our place in the world as less problematic than the first Quakers did in the seventeenth century, and may feel our faith and our Quakerism as optional, non-essential preferences rather than prerequisites for a faithful life. However, even from this perspective, we sit within a tradition which has always refused to be confined to collective devotions without effects beyond the meeting house. It is not about having a spiritual life with consequences, it is about the spiritual life containing within it the response of prayer within worship and prayerful practice outside of formal worship: our Quaker faith has always understood itself as being about the whole of life. 'I cannot separate my life from being a Quaker.'

'I am a Quaker, completely, I don't think of it as a belief, it is just the way that I am, it's how I am, … it's my identity, it is not about deciding you're a Quaker, it is about realising you're a Quaker.'

Even as we are left to choose how to interpret what our Quaker faith may look like most of the time, it is still a task we have to face. So, in our daily lives we may live in smaller houses than our peers, drive smaller cars or none at all, and own fewer things. We may be invisible as Quakers in a landscape of increasing consumer and environmental awareness but are highly self-aware and self-questioning. And our fundamental reasons for our Quaker concerns are spiritually based, not born out of secular humanism. My own Quaker life now contains within it many of the concerns and consequences of my earlier life as an anarchist but now I act out of God's love within me, not a secular celebration of a particular ideology. It is not about acting now for this life is all we have, but acting now because it is God's time to act, for my generation and the next.

It is about our lives being ones of 'becoming'. We are never just a Quaker (as others are not just a Muslim) but we are striving always to be the better person of faith, the more obedient, the more faithful, the more aware. Faith is about becoming. 'Peace starts with us – I am the only person I can change … God works with us as individual souls.' We work on our lives, 'letting the Light in, not dwelling on the darkness' and we support each other: 'to be out there in the world doing this as a small group is hard, knowing that you're not wasting your time or dwelling on irrelevancies.' Some of us feel we don't easily fit into society. Not coming to meeting can increase that sense of alienation or make us less thoughtful in our choices. Coming to meeting can make us more aware of 'problems and injustices' but also give us support to do the things we feel we need to.

This sense of always 'becoming' is simply a fact of God's invitation in our lives. We are not Quakers because we are good, but because we are not. God loves us in spite of ourselves and we respond because of how we are. And we become more towards on our journey of faith. More congruent.

And, as Jesus' teachings tell us, worry does not add one moment to our life, one measure to our life's journey. Worry is the opposite of faith. It is focused on particulars, built on notions, and has no room for the spectacular and that which is not yet known, the focus of hope in Romans 8. Faith takes us we know not where but the destination is unimportant, the process of being led and following faithfully is all. God will take us where we need to go and 'the big picture will emerge in time', a glimpse or reflection of the republic of heaven. Worry takes up energy and time so much more usefully spent on the fruits of discipleship, testimony to the grace of God acting in our lives now and calling us out to help others and to help create a just and peaceful world.

Quakers 'celebrate life, life as it can be for everybody.' We have 'a way of life, not a religion' and we 'have to be prepared to live it, to keep it in mind all the time.' There is so much to celebrate: 'sincerity, the involvement of everybody', 'the respect given children', 'testimony and the expectations and values that go with that, silence, meeting, worship, the direct line to God, that questions are okay, encouraged'. We are part of a tradition of people trying to achieve greater justice in the world and we have also had great moments of corporate insight and action that spur us on in our present-day attempts to change the world. And taking action is simple.

'Our meeting had received an appeal for work with children in Madagascar and we were oohing and aahing about whether to send money and how much and then Gabriel, seven, ministered. He suggested the children's meeting could bake biscuits and sell them to help send money to the children. This has now become a regular activity but part of our meeting life still led by the young people.'

The emphasis of our testimony today is on justice through simplicity and moderation, peace, integrity, care of creation, and the nurture of community. Testimony is expression. Quakers are not 'for peace' but rather know, in the deepest sense of the word, that peace is a holy imperative as part of a just society. We do not prefer peace or campaign for peace in isolation from a whole lot of other issues, rather we have imbibed God's loving purposes in their simplicity and totality. We inhabit our testimony. It is both straightforward and enormously far-reaching. It is simple but total. It is, as it always has been for Quakers, about turning the world upside down. We never forget that: we cannot sit in our meetings without taking on the world and values that lie beyond and against our experience of God.

It is not ultimately about words but about experience. Our testimony is what we do from our experience of God, not what we say. Testimony is not creed but action. This is the same as faith because the two are inseparable. Testimony is only faith in action. It is all of our lives as well as all those things we do together as Quakers. It is wonderfully simple and simply wonderful.

We are Quakers.

Reflection and discussion

The following questions are designed to help you reflect on your own experience of what you value and celebrate about being a Quaker.

They can be used either for individual reflection, or by small groups. If you are meeting as a group, agree some ground rules at the beginning. Important ones might be to allow everyone a chance to speak, to speak only from your own experience, and that no-one has to speak if they don't want to.

Make sure that the book and the questions are accessible to anyone not able to read print, either by obtaining an audio version or reading relevant sections aloud in the group.

If the group is large, you may wish to spend some time in twos, threes or fours before returning to the large group.

Choose between worship sharing or group discussion. Groups may prefer one or the other. Some dislike the discipline of worship sharing when they are bursting with ideas; some find it difficult to contribute to a discussion if they are not given a specific space to do so. Be sensitive to everyone's needs.

Questions for reflection and celebration

1. What do you celebrate about being a Quaker?

2. What are the gifts given to you? What is your unique role in your Quaker community? What is your ministry? How do you affirm it?

3. How can we nurture openness to the magic and grace of God's love in our Meetings?

4. What dreams can we discern for the future? What is your vision for the future of Quaker community? What is the next step for you towards this vision?

5. What is your experience of discernment? What moves you from concern to action? In what ways is your life one of 'becoming'?

6. How do we live our Quakerism more overtly? How do we realise 'the kingdom' in our lives? With others? In our Meetings? In the wider community?